AGAINST LINEARITY

EARL McKENZIE

AGAINST LINEARITY

PEEPAL TREE

First published in Great Britain in 1992
Peepal Tree Books
17, King's Avenue
Leeds LS6 1QS
Yorkshire
England

ISBN 0 948833 63 7

Acknowledgements

Some of the poems selected have appeared in *Bim, Jamaica Journal, The Sunday Gleaner, Savacou, The Graham House Review, Crossing Water*, and *Prism International*.

CONTENTS

THE BLUE STONES OF MY RIVER

I know that I shall never be at peace again
with the blue stones of my river,
stones washed by centuries of rain
out of the hills around me;

stones at the bottom of the river,
cool in the heat of the sun,
basking in the shimmering light.

I have seen the mist of the valley
floating over them,
angels of fog
walking over the monuments.

I have seen them at the edge
of the chasm,
darker than fear;
and I have been the first to see them
on mornings younger
than the optimism of birds.

I have sat on those stones,
canopied by roseapple and trumpet trees,
and felt the water
gouge the land beside my feet.

The blue stones of my river
have sunken lower now,
and I know that I shall never touch
their surfaces again.

FIREFLY

Even if with some reluctance,
I will, first thing in the morning,
flush a cockroach found loitering
in the sink;
and this was what I thought I had done
until a light appeared in the dark hole.

Quickly I fished the firefly out:
you do not drown such a beautiful thing.

I held him between my fingers,
watched his head mechanically ticking,
watched his headlights fade in the light.

I took him over to my bookshelf
and slipped him into the darkness
behind some heavy books,
hoping he would rest.

But he emerged at once
with his lights beaming,
and he crawled up the back
of a book on moral problems.

I took him outside
and put him on the grass,
but he was even more uneasy
in the morning sun;
his glory is to flash through forests
on the darkest nights.

So I piled up a stack of leaves
beside a wall,
and placing him
between darkness and light,
left it up to him.

THE NEVER-DIE TREES ARE BLOSSOMING

for Adlyn

The never-die trees are blossoming,
and I drive under a canopy
of their blue immortality.

These never-die trees are fence posts,
but their sky-blue flowers
have nothing to do
with keeping cattle in.

These trees are the blooming walls
of a jail,
but this celebration with flowers
is older than cattle pens
and the bondage of barbed wire.

These blossoms come
from free flowing juices;
these flowers are crying out
for the full freedom of trees.

PICKING UP AVOCADOS

for Gillian

The path I followed every day
crossed the place where the avocados fell;
I picked them up and took them home,
gave some to my friends.

It was the tree's yearly hope
for future generations;
the blossoms came unnoticed,
the young fruits grew without my attention.

Now at the brink of ripeness, they fell
covering the crossroads.

Some fell among rocks
scattering slivers of new moons;
some fell on hardened soil and broke
with fragments clinging to their seeds;
some fell on gentler surfaces
and rolled unmarked,
settled in the dewy grass.

And I, an unthinking part of the plan,
picked up the goblets of ripening butter
and scattered the seeds.

BEAUTY SPOT

There is a place
on the other side of a river
where the erosion of rock
has formed a sculpture
of the female organ of love.

Trucks and buses of holiday makers
stop to look at it.

Men and women laugh together
and many surprising things are said.

Children stand at the wall and look,
sensing that they are at the brink
of a great mystery.

Then the travellers resume their journey,
marvelling that nature
should have made such a thing.

DEATH OF A DOG

Men know they will die,
make preparations,
cushion their deaths
with soft answers
for hard
flesh-bruising questions.

But dogs, I am told,
meet death with surprise,
are ambushed by its fierce
and unrelenting power.

Their suffering is purest pain
unrelieved by reflective
questionings.

His beginning and his end
are now fused
in the funeral mud
I wipe from my shoes.

And I who must think
ponder my burning link
in the chain of suffering.

THIS ANIMAL OF FUNERALS

This animal of funerals
does not let go of its dead
searches for their bones
in faraway fields of war
holds on to them
with cenotaph, tomb or urn.

Observe the rites with which
  the bonds are forged;
Heed the griefs and all the tears
  that have flowed;
Study the libraries where their
  names are preserved;
Notice the wreaths on the monuments
  of every age
Saying that the dead
  are our heritage.

Animal of symbol, spirit,
  whatever else you call us,
We are also *homo funeralicus*.

MOTHER AND CHILD

The donkey standing
in the middle of the road
refused to give way to our car;
I braked and veered
to the edge of the road,
this would be a slow
and careful passing.

But soon it was clear
this was no mere animal
caught in the middle of a crossing:
for she looked as if she was there
long before we were born,
and the stillness of the night before,
and the stillness of the morning
hung heavily on her.

This is not a highway,
something in her manner said,
this is the earth.

And then I saw her dead child
lying at her feet,
flattened by the wheels of traffic
into a silhouette,
yet with its youthful features
undestroyed,
and now mounted
like a bas relief
on the paved surface
of our civilisation.

Framed in my rear-view mirror
a mother and child
in the middle of an empty highway;
framed in my rear-view mirror
a mother donkey standing on the earth,
oblivious to our passing.

AWAKENING

Among hard and unfriendly bodies
I am a stranger wondering
why I am here,
then I turn and see her face.
The crowd disappears
and I hear my soul saying:
she is the one,
look carefully at her.

The crowd returns,
hard cold bodies jostling,
and the rough waves
sweep her away.

The crowd disappears
and I hear my soul saying:
I have showed her to you
and the long held promise
has been kept.
It is the end of your waiting
and the beginning
of your understanding.

A LOVE OF HILLS AND PLAINS

You like my hills
and I like your plains.

My hills have private peaks
you can climb to
through bamboo walks
and blossoming gungo peas.

You can nibble roseapples on the way,
sit for a while on sweet-potato hills,
savour each hillful of cosy spirituality.

Then you can sit on their tops
and in the exhilaration of their heights
contemplate rivers, fields and sky.

Come to my hills.

Your plains are fragrant with robin mangoes,
hot as pea-soup and aboriginal as bammies;
They are as nourishing as cashews,
and as spicy as peppered shrimps.

For your culture of work,
wholesome as savannah mulch
I often go down to see
your water-colour farms
of melon and escallion
sloping to where the sea
dances on its sandy stage.

And you come from those plains,
you with complexion sweet as logwood honey
and eyes like their brown fields.

I am coming to your plains.

EVENING

Driving from the beach
we saw the sunset
flashing through the trees
and gilding the edges
of breadfruit leaves.

We saw the sunset's yellow
blending with the hue
of ripe papaws.

We passed a tree of white egrets.

And we saw twin rainbows,
the first in our lives,
hanging in the sky
in front of us.

Twin rainbows: one for her
and one for me;
and between us,
four pots of gold.

WOMAN

I grew from you
Like a fruit from a tree
Independent now
Yet carrying you
In unrecognised regions
Of my mind.

And I am a slave to you still
For I worship you in my heart
And I admire you on streets
And on buses

And I search for the secret you have
You who in your weakness
Reduce me to the absence of all strength
And urge me on forever
To the release of a kind of death
And birth
In your arms.

PICTURES

My body draws pictures of her
while I sleep.

Sometimes it colours her
with blues and sepias,
and she is light,
almost immaterial.

And sometimes she is three-dimensional
and sharper and clearer than life.

She rises up from somewhere,
and we are in a kiss
that had no beginning

and ends when my eyes open
to the light of the room.

Sometimes I see her watching me,
but she does not speak.

And there are times
when I see her jostling crowds
at unexpected places.

But most of all
there is this kiss
that had no beginning
but which nevertheless ends.

CUPS

We drank from our pair of cups,
yours with delicate tones of cream
and grey,
mine a deep unspeckled green,
and both with a band of brown
that linked us.

In the aura of our mornings
we held them with our affection
still warm in our fingers;
and we sipped from them
with the sweetness
of the night's understandings
still on our lips.

Now you cannot drink from yours,
and I will not drink from mine alone;
so these silent witnesses
of our journey to each other
sit together
in a dark cupboard.

MY WISE OLD LAMP

The books on my shelf
cast a shadow on the wall
forming a silhouette of a city.

The light from my desk lamp
strikes the familiar titles;
these are books I have read.

But the city skyline on the wall
has gone unnoticed all this time;
I've been too busy with new volumes.

And all these nights my wise old lamp
has been projecting this ancient parable
on my room's small screen.

Shaping from old and well-worn tomes
a new and untravelled place,
a tempting metropolis of shadow.

These new volumes sprawled on my desk
will add to that widening skyline;
we always leave unexplored cities behind.

But unread books also cast their cities:
we may tour their waterfronts, go deep into the town,
but their streets will be different tomorrow.

Tonight this everlasting place of the unread,
this magnetic skyline, beckons with the purity
of all unlived in artifice.

SCULPTURE AMONG PALM TREES

I dream of civilisation in hot sunlight:
of poetry on beaches
and sculpture among palm trees.

And I dream of music played
by those who touch this land
and caress its blades of grass
with love in their fingers.

HILL PEOPLE

To ascend or descend
is nearly the only choice
of motion here;
and erect bodies with loads
of hard traditions
on their heads
move up and down
in their slow and strenuous
dance
on the land's exacting
curvature.

Few remember now
that seen from slavery's
lowlands,
this stiff and stony soil
was once a dream
that soothed broken bodies.

And while they fashion
new wishes
from their toils in this place,
from this first chance
so ardently taken,
these feet which
are descended
from feet which survived
chains and treadmills,
continue to write
their signatures of tracks
across the stern land's
crumpled surfaces.

THE OLD COTTON TREES ARE DYING

The old cotton trees are
dying in this land
where the young grow
the locks and beards of the old
and do not plant trees.
The oldtime people used to say
these canoe trees
these coffin trees
are the dwelling places
of our spirits.

We make these objects of
travelling
from the largest trees in
our land.

I have studied history
in the thick buttresses of
their roots,
in their ancient beards of cotton,
and in the generations
of orchids and cacti
growing on their branches.

Now the old cotton trees are dying
and I wonder if the spirits
are scattered.

DOWN THE GULLY

We lived on things
that came from
down the gully.

We dipped into it
for water and fish from the rivers;
crops from the ground;
wild fruits from the trees.

You never knew
what our gully would yield:
cucumbers with firewood
breadfruits and dry coconuts
soursops and sugar cane.

Once it was my wonderland:
some mornings it was a lake of mist
before the sunrise on the mountain top
cleared up the valley's mysteries;
there I trapped pea-doves in calabans,
learned that black crows had white chickens,
and admired the geometry of yam hills.
Then I learned that
down the gully
was a place of labour;
my father went down in the morning,
my mother carried his lunch in a carrier,
he came up
in the sunset's shadow.

My father is dead now
and the last time we spoke
he lamented the decline in his fields
down the gully.

Now bushes grow
among the cocoa trees
in our gully.

A TALE OF TWO TONGUES

Miss Ida speaks only English to God.
Scholars cannot fault the diction
of her graces and prayers;
to her, it is the language of holy things;
and the giver of commandments
deserves a grammar of respectability
as firm and as polished
as his tablets of stone.

But to fellow mortals she speaks Creole,
the tongue of the markets and the fields;
the language of labrish,
su-su, proverbs and stories,
hot-words, tracings and preckeh;
it is the way to get
hard-ears pickney to listen
and facety men to keep off;
it is the tongue of belly laughs
and sweet body action.

And to Miss Ida it is no bother
to laugh and suffer in one language
and worship in another.

BACKROW TRAVELLERS

With religious sadness in their eyes
they sit in the solemnity of pews.

Sometimes they float like saints
above the smoke of hell-fire
blowing in our eyes.

They observe us with the gravity
of members of a jury.

We watch them
until we overtake
the silent stoicism
of their truths.

CHURCH BELLS

Two church bells rang in separate villages
One a baptist bass
The other a methodist soprano
and every Sunday morning
I heard them ringing together.

Most people who lived near the baptist bell
Went to the methodist church,
And those from the methodist village
Heeded the baptist call.

They met each other on the way
Going separate ways to heaven.

THE SINGING RASTAS

I met a truckload of singing Rastas
Coming around a bend, going downhill.

It was a bearded choir on wheels
Going to their convention, someone said.

Black apostolic faces, mellow, pious eyes
Looking over the wings; they were singing heartily.

This was not a song required by captors,
Not reggae mirth required by those who wasted them.

They had already taken down their harps
From roseapple trees by the rivers of Babylon.

And the strains of the song that now came to me
Was a sorrow-laden yet fighting melody.

THREE STARES

mule hauling sustenance of man
skin burnt with whip and sun
tired hoofs slithering on parched asphalt
foam rising endlessly in its tortured mouth
eyes pained and wild
eyes staring without comprehension

goat with all legs tied
falls from bicycle bar
falls heavily to the ground
no movement to break the fall
falls on sharp edges of stones
looks up and bleats
bleats to traffic noises
and rough surrounding voices
raises its head and stares
stares without comprehension

dog scouring the road for food
feels rock of schoolboy in its side
whelps turns and flees
flees shower of pelting stones
stops at the curb and turns
turns and through its bleeding eyes
stares without comprehension

THIS DAY

. . . i emerged in a cold sweat
haunted by the pained faces
of dead arawaks
and sick to the stomach
from the stench of slavers
and the sounds of black men crying

i came away trembling
from the bloody blades of pirates
the cruel stares of gold-hungry eyes
and the blasts of cannon shots

i turned away distressed
by human blood on bluest seas
by horrors coiled in greenest grass
by gods so twisted and so shamed
by dreams that challenged setting suns
yet dreams so wet with blood

i came and knelt with grateful knees
before the slightest good that did prevail
i came and sought some comfort in the thought
of happier childhoods laid
beneath those layers of pain

And now I dare not die beside that poisoned chrysalis
Before I force a better judgement on this day. . .

POLITICAL INK

On a clear, cool morning
I dipped my finger in the ink,
lost my political innocence.

I put my first mark on a ballot
and unknowingly
joined forces
with a chilling majority.

The day after,
some who voted like me
were stoned to death
had their houses burned.

Some who voted like me
burned effigies
performed macabre mock rituals
of death and burial.

On a clear, cool morning
fresh with the sunrise
I dipped my finger
in the political ink
and lost my innocence.

AFTER THE ELECTION

After the election
a car with loudspeakers
brings a tape-recorded
thank-you message
to the people.

It drives over
patchy campaign asphalt
recently laid;
passes painted slogans
which once dripped prophetically,
like blood.

A small shop smothered by posters
clings timidly
to the road's uncompromising edge.
Inside, sweaty customers turn
from rising prices
to watch the deception pass.

The disembodied voice,
mockingly amplified,
briefly stills the sounds
of hoes chopping earth
as farmers scramble to the road.
They stand in a row
and glare their silent resentment
at the grinning henchmen
working the winner's machine.

Toddlers follow mothers to gates,
and school children turn
from their teacher's unrealities
to stare through classroom windows
at another.

In a valley,
a woman now nine times pregnant,
and washing clothes by a riverside,
hears her candidate's voice and smiles.

But an old woman in a rocking chair
receives the news without surprise,
and without comment,
rocks as she has rocked for years.

BURGLAR BARS

Burglar bars have become an art form
In our nervous land.

The masters of this renaissance of dread,
Work in studios with apprentices:
They work late at night
Designing patterns of steel,
Elegant geometries
And shapes of plants and animals
To keep the burglars out.

For a price they build pretty cages for our privacy
And tombs for our freedom.

Not ours are pyramids to the dead,
Not cathedrals with stained glass windows.
Not totem poles for our ancestors;

But metal ornaments against evil,
Visual harmonies for the burglar's eyes,
And sculpted elegance for his philistine hands.

Only cold metallic webs of beauty
Stand between us and the night.

DANCING WITH STRANGERS

I have danced
with too many strangers,
watched their bodies
gyrating in front of me,
eyes averted
minds stunned by the beat.

I have danced with strangers
without knowing their views on
nuclear weapons
capital punishment
and aid to the poor.

I have danced with strangers
when they were
my tenuous hold on others
while I dangled
over the chasm
of the insanity of dancing alone.

Dancing with strangers
can make you sick
when there is no shared
meaning in the movement
and the rhythm is the pounding out
of your isolation
and there is no harmony
of body
or heart.

THE LYNCHING

Someone
called a passing stranger
a thief,

and farmers
who sing on choirs,

and basket makers
who like sturdy frames,

and wives
who hug husbands,

and unemployed youths
who once made music
from sweetcups,

and young women
with milk for babies
in their breasts,

turned into a mob
and beat the stranger
to death.

PETCHARY

There was a petchary eating peppers
on the tree beneath the window.

I had seen them in the sky
Peppering hawks—
A small bird screeching and assailing
Sending the big bird of prey fleeing.

Now a petchary close-up
With his black head
And bulging, aggressive brow,

I sensed his audacity,
and belligerence;
Less than an arm's length away
This chaser of hawks.
Devouring hot peppers.

AFTER THE HURRICANE, THE MOON

After the hurricane, the moon
poured its gold over the rubble.

From our roofless house,
now without TV,
we watched it rising
on the sky's screen.

It told a story
of beauty after terror
of gentle light like oil
on our wounds.

The storm destroyed
and the moon rose
both going their way
in nature's indifference.

But we who watched
from our shattered house
felt both blasted and blessed.

FLINT

The day after the rain,
during the retaliation of the sun,
the land broke.

Yam
potato
and cassava
fields

slid
down
the hillside.

Birds and butterflies flew into the air.

Earthworms, frogs and mongooses
mingled with colliding flint stones.

Sparks struck dry guava leaves,
darted into tossing guinea grass.

And when the land was still again

the flames spread out,
climbed vines into bamboo groves,
ran along fallen branches into cane fields,
and proclaimed their conquest from the tops of trees.

Later in the village people cried
and searched their lives for sins.

And in the night
the sounds of singing and drumming
were blown by the wind
across the moonlit fields
of ashes and dust.

COFFEE BLOSSOMS IN THE BLUE MOUNTAINS

for Ezona

Here with mountain peaks for neighbours
and deep valleys full of silence
I breathe a cool and mystic air.

And I see coffee blossoms
on the green side of a mountain.

They are like snow
sprinkled by a huge hand
that swung over the mountain tops.

I picked a good day to visit,
they tell me,
one of the two or three in the year
when coffee blossoms appear.

Tomorrow they fade and the trees
concentrate
on making black coffee
from white blossoms.

SABBATH

Now, perhaps only once a week,
laughter comes from deep down
with force enough to crack
and briefly displace
the accumulated lava
of your pains.

And when it comes
it shakes the ruins of your world
and old plaster falls from the roofs.

And the air has the smell
of freshly fallen rain.

And while it lasts.
You have a clearer view of things.

Hold on to this moment
For it is your sabbath.

ARAWAK DRAWINGS

We stood beneath them
With minds submitted to the communication
Of dark symbols speaking from another age.

The cave might have been a casual studio
On a day when heavy rains
Forced the mind to introspection
And to fancy.

Or perhaps that quiet cleft
Was the dwelling place of imagined spirits;
spirits controlled by the power
Of that artist's hand.

And today
When they are no longer here
Their simple drawings speak for them
In a remote gallery of rock.

THE MAKERS

My parents were makers.

My father made houses and coffins,
sheltered both life and death.

Home owners and the once bereaved
came to pay him homage when he died;
I learned the worth of his hands
from the testimony of their eyes.

My mother plaited straw,
made hats and mats.
This was the skill, she said,
that schooled me.

Her ageing hands plait straw no more,
I watch them resting on her lap,
hands that plaited my fate.

Today I make this poem
for my parents, the makers.

A COCONUT ALPHABET

I

The coconut has answers
Answers like the mustard seed.

The coconut has answers of its own
Answers locked in husk and shell
Concealed in hues of green.

Answers that grow and die,
Tall strong answers;

Answers in its shapes
And answers in its rhythms.

The coconut has answers of its own
Like the lilies of the field.

II

It is as if there is embedded in its seed
A greater longing for the sun
A greater need to live with clouds
A greater need to pierce blue emptiness.

III

It climbs the sky
With the rhythmic pattern
Of a reggae beat in silvery grey.

A curved syncopation on blue
With a radial finale of fronds
    that explodes
In a crescendo of splintered green.

This is the silent
Organic rocketry
Of many years.

This is a botanical exploration
Of outer space.

IV

When the wind blows
The eyes expect
The slender trunk to break
But the visual strength deceives.

When the wind blows
An inverted pendulum
With a shattered head
Moves in slow motion.

When the wind blows
There are cones, circles and ovals
In my mind.

V

The
earth
pulls
a
nut
from
its
stem
and
the
green
meteor
falls
to a quick collision on the grass;

it rolls a bit
                    and
                    tumbles
                    and
                    pitchpupalick!
                    pitchpupalick!
                    pitchpupalick!
                    to equilibrium.

VI

By their fruits they shall be known
And by this fruit we might discover
Some aspects of the truth.

Ripe yellow green declares
The fruit is not yet dry;
Three firm bulges
And a hollow at the top;
And now a steady shake reveals
The pleasant chuckle of untasted juice.

Ripe coconut feels the chop of my machete
My thirsty hunger tears the husk away
Top pattern
Like
Bottom pattern
My uncaring thirst is not concerned
Ripe coconut feels the front and back
of my machete.

Nut.
Hard nut.
Beautifully textured nut.

Hard nut feels the chop of my machete
I meet the gaping
Nectar water
Milky blue and sweet
And by this taste of liquid life
my gulping thirst is drowned.

VII

Then with a brush I tried to find
What with machete I did not discover
And soon coconut shapes began to say
Uncoconut things to me
And I found innumerable letters
locked within a coconut alphabet.

A man can become a coconut tree
and with nuts for words
Speak bunches.

VIII

And the structure of my days cannot be free
Of the imprints of the coconut tree
For I have climbed the patterns of its trunk
And felt the light of sun and moon.

For I have lived in nuts and husks
And have wandered around in kernels;

And I have felt the force of blues and greens
And have dreamt of patterns

Golden coconut patterns
Etched in the blue of night.

AGAINST LINEARITY

We reject the straight line.

We crowd and push
and use our elbows
at the entrances
of buses, post offices
and movie theatres.

Our motorists break
the unbroken white line
and overtake the overtaker.

A minibus driver
shouts jumbled destinations,
and his route
is the web
of an anarchist spider.

Our rebels idolise Knotty Dread
for knotty is the way
to Jah and Zion.

We fear the straight line
for it is as rigid as death.

Those who know its power
respect its slide-rule
secrets of accomplishment.

Others want to bend it
into trees and rivers
into the crookedness of life.

NOON AND MIDNIGHT

A taxi driver laughs
as he runs over a dog
in Jamaica.

Children burn alive
while party opponents
block the fire brigade
in Jamaica.

A Rastaman smokes the herb
then throws himself
in the lion's den
in Jamaica.

Jamaica is midnight
Jamaica is noon
Jamaica is midnight
Jamaica is noon.

A schoolgirl dressed
in white and blue
wears a red hibiscus
in her hair
in Jamaica.

A smiling fruitseller
who has no change
tells me to pay
when I pass again
in Jamaica.

Peasant fathers
of famous sons
head for their farms
first sign of day
in Jamaica.

Jamaica is midnight
Jamaica is noon
Jamaica is midnight
Jamaica is noon

Jamaica, spare us
your poisoned
midnight calabash.

Jamaica, with your
clear noon water
cool our flaming tongues.

Earl McKenzie was born in Mount Charles, in the parish of St. Andrew, Jamaica in 1943. He attended Oberlin High School and Mico Teachers' College. He was awarded a first degree at Columbia University and a doctorate from the University of British Columbia. He has taught in Jamaican high schools and at Church Teacher's College. He is currently lecturing in philosophy at the University of the West Indies, Mona, Jamaica.

His other publications include: *A Boy Named Ossie: A Jamaican Childhood* and *Two Roads to Mount Joyful and other Stories*.